A patient's disease is a caregivers "dis-ease"

~Dr. Monica Hardy

CAREGIVERS: The Forgotten Patient
Emotional Support for Alzheimer's Caregivers
By: Monica Hardy, EdD, DMin, MA, RHIA

For further information, please contact Dr. Monica Hardy by visiting
www.drmonicahardy.com

Distributed by E'fek-tiv Enterprises Publishing
Ingram Sparks Platform
Printed in the United States of America

Copyright © 2023

Cover Design and Graphics by MRF Graphics and Music, LLC
Michael Fuller

Edited by Dwan Thomas
HIM Professional Excel

Cartoon Illustrations by Farrah Milan
www.farrahmilan.com

ISBN: 979-8-218-19874-9

Any Biblical Scriptures used were taken from BibleGateway.com via The King James Version, The New International Version, The Message Bible, or The Amplified Bible.

ABOUT THE COVER

The cover of this book is purple because purple is the color for Alzheimer's Awareness month. The cover represents how empty, exhausted, and depleted a caregiver gets after a trying day. The word patient does not only mean a person under medical care; it also means undergoing the action of another and bearing provocation, annoyance, misfortune, delay, hardship, and pain.

SPECIAL INSTRUCTIONS

Before every emotion, you will find my cartoon illustration and a caption. This represents what my thoughts and emotions were as a caregiver-- things I could not or simply did not want to verbalize. If the cartoon makes you laugh, good! I give you permission to laugh, cry and do whatever makes you feel better. I started writing this book while taking care of my dad, and it was the grumpy cartoon characters or ones with interesting personalities like: Yosemite Sam®, The Grinch®, Charlie Brown®, Squidward®, Jack-Jack from the Incredibles®, Anger®, Grumpy Smurf®, Grumpy Dwarf®, Grumpy Care Bear®, Tasmanian Devil®, Wile E. Coyote®, and Roz of Monsters, Inc. ® that provided me with a much needed release. Unfortunately, I could not get the rights to use these characters in the book. Nevertheless, in every emotional chapter, I will mention one of these characters because their expressions brought me comical relief. At times, I could not find comfort in the words of people because all they could see was my dad and his pain. So, this book allowed me to just say it through expressions! After you read these captions and read my story, feel empowered to journal your stories. Write exactly how you feel or felt. Tell the whole truth so help you God, and guess what? When you are done, you are still a good person, a great provider, and a loving caregiver.

Disclaimer
LISTEN CAREFULLY

<u>The caregiver loves in another language!</u>

This book was not all that easy to write, but I truly believe it is necessary to read, especially if you are a caregiver.

Doctors, scientists, specialists, researchers, etc., may read this book and automatically start analyzing, explaining, justifying, or rationalizing the behaviors mentioned.

Let me make this very clear; this book is a VOICE, ADVOCATE and OUTLET FOR CAREGIVERS!

Everyone can read this book, but everyone will not understand this language of love, especially if you are not a caregiver.

DEDICATION

I pray this book is a masterpiece so you can master peace!

I dedicate this handbook to CAREGIVERS all over the world. Whether you are caring for a loved one with Alzheimer's or another unkind disease, I want you to know you are not alone. You are appreciated. Your sacrifices have not gone un-noticed, and a dose of love and laughter will help you make it through another day.

I also dedicate this handbook to my beloved daddy, the late Willie Hardy Sr., my brother, the late Willie Hardy Jr., and his companion Takecia Hardy. Our care for dad not only brought about varied, unexpected emotions but also showed us the importance of love and laughter.

ACKNOWLEDGMENTS

I HONOR my HEAVENLY Father

Lord, I thank you for loving me. Lord, I thank you for your grace and mercy and for being patient with me when I did not understand my dad and was unable to be patient. Lord, thank you for answering my dad's prayers to give him a daughter. Lord, thank you that the daughter you gave him was me. Although there were many times I did not think I was cut out to care for my dad and wanted to abandon the assignment, I thank you for seeing me through. Lord, I thank you for the many years you allowed my dad to live and for the time I got to spend with my dad. Lord, I thank you for your safety and protection over my dad. I thank you for not allowing my dad to fall, hurt himself, poison himself or wander into harm's way. Lord, thank you for allowing me to never see my dad's flaws while he was healthy, because I now only have the disease to blame.

I HONOR my NATURAL Father

Dad, I know you are now with God, but thank you for asking God to give you a daughter. I know you did not know it would be me, but I'm so blessed that it was me. Thank you for being a strong disciplinarian. Thank you for telling me I was cute and securing my self-esteem at a young age. Thank you for treasuring me, spoiling me, protecting me and being my HERO. Thank you for setting a standard in my life for how a man should work and provide for his family. Finally, thank you for showing me unconditional love. Although this disease brought out the worst and best in both of us, my love for you grew stronger every day as we weathered daily storms trying to understand life with this dis-ease!

Willie L Hardy Sr.

My Beloved Dad & Hero
1943-2020

A SPECIAL THANK YOU

I THANK my son, Jairus, for being my relief as a caregiver. We played tag and took turns caring for dad, which was not an easy task. I would also like to THANK my son, TJ, you could not be around as much but did what you could while at home.

I THANK my Auntie Betty, Uncle Sidney, and Uncle Lucious (departed in 2017), for stopping by to see dad, sit with dad, or take dad out so I could have a break.

I THANK Lasheala Holloway, Cedric Williams Jr., Terrell Simmons, Austin Lee, Warren and Martha McDaniels, Adrian Long, and Brianna Buggs for stepping in to help transport and care for dad in both Jacksonville and Orlando.

I THANK my bestie, Dwan Thomas for being by my side and for editing this book. I am blessed to have a best friend that is a professional writer and editor.

I THANK my Godson, Alvin Barlow Jr., for simply being there. Your calls and our talks are priceless.

I THANK Apostle Tammy Reese for telling me funny stories from when your loved one was living with this disease. Thank you for prophesying to me that I was going to write about this to help others.

I THANK Bertha Barrett for being my mental health counselor and an objective sounding board.

I THANK Dr. Ane Mercer for defending dad, cooking for dad, and for also planning a getaway for me to relax.

I THANK Dr. Carolyn Love for helping me with resources for dad's long-term care needs.

I THANK Vicki Farrie for unknowingly calling in the moment of a breakdown but patiently listening and responding with the appropriate words or song (especially on dads 77th birthday).

I THANK Apostle Chantell Poole, of all the chaplains that could have come, God sent you to stand with me, pray with me and provide counsel.

I THANK Gwendolyn McNeil for sitting with my dad and for the daily calls and texts to check on me.

I THANK Wilma Allen for calling and texting to check on me, for giving me insight based on your knowledge as a nursing home caregiver and for bringing me chai tea from Panera Bread.

I THANK Apostle Alva Harris, Pastor Ida Harris, Ambassador Lorraine Chavis, Mary Peterson, and my Deliverance Temple family for assisting me, showing compassion, and praying.

I THANK my wealth and business coach, Gerald D. Rogers. After suffering much loss and trauma, you refused to let me recluse or give up. Thank you for sharing wisdom on how to go to the next level as an entrepreneur. I appreciate you uplifting, inspiring, empowering, and pushing me to go forward in business and book publishing.

I THANK my cartoon illustrator, Farrah Milan. From the moment I met you and shared my vision, you grabbed hold to it with both hands. Your energy pushed me to want to do what I wasn't sure how to do and that is to place this book in the hands of caregivers all over the world.

I THANK my graphic artist, Michael Fuller. You have worked with me on a number of book covers and you never disappoint. This year, you have taken on so much more with the internal graphics and marketing. Once again, you never disappoint.

I THANK my business associate, Lee Von Nuttall. You have worked with me on a number of book projects. Thank you for taking time to help with the publishing side of my authorpreneurship.

I THANK everyone that asked about my dad or showed compassion for my dad. Although I had moments where I was not feeling supported, you helped me by showing me caregivers feel and think differently AND this book was needed.

**If for any reason you played a part in my life as a support aid and I failed to thank you, <u>PLEASE FORGIVE ME</u>. Writing this book was more challenging than I realized. I started writing when my dad and my brother were alive, and they are now both gone. Despite the tears that fell as I recalled these memories; it was all I could do to keep from breaking down hysterically. Please know that you are very much appreciated.

FOREWORD

Alzheimer's disease is a progressive neurodegenerative disorder of the brain. It affects memory, language, and overall thinking. An estimated 6.5 million Americans, age 65 and older, are living with Alzheimer's dementia. 1 in 9 people, age 65 and older, has Alzheimer's dementia.[1] A person lives an average of four to eight years with Alzheimer's dementia, but some live up to 20 years. There is currently no cure, and it is inherently progressive. Therefore, overtime, a person living with Alzheimer's disease will require more and more assistance with activities of daily living (ADLs). The burden of this disease not only affects the individual, but also to their families and caregivers.

Caregivers are likely to be one or more family members. In 2012, caregivers provided an estimated 16 billion hours of informal assistance.[1] It is truly a family disease. As a caregiver for someone with Alzheimer's disease, you are likely to face a range of emotions, from fear and frustration to love and joy. There will be many things you will not understand. It can be overwhelming to adjust to the changes that come with caring for someone with Alzheimer's, and it is normal to feel like you are in a roller coaster of emotions. Your emotions should not be explained away, minimized, or forgotten.

It is not an easy job, but it is an incredibly important one. As you care for your loved one, you are doing something that is meaningful and has a lasting impact. This book will be a source of insight and validation for you as you continue to care for your loved one with Alzheimer's disease. Mr. Hardy had several physicians, but I was his very first Neurologist and I am honored to have been his healthcare provider. I have been with this family from the beginning of this journey, and I am proud of my sister-friend, Dr. Monica Hardy in completing this much needed literary project. According to Brett H. Lewis, *"Doctors diagnose, nurses heal, and caregivers make sense of it all"*.

Kalina Sanders, MD
Board Certified Neurologist
Baptist Neurology – Jacksonville

1. Alzheimer's Association. 2022 Alzheimer's Disease Facts and Figures. Alzheimer's Dement 2022,18.

TABLE OF CONTENTS

INTRODUCTION
My dad, my life's hero, had Alzheimer's

 My dad has always been tempered, but growing up I never saw much because my mom hid his flaws. Unfortunately, this disease caused his attitude and all his imperfections to come into the light in a "not-so-positive" fashion. Dad was very independent, prideful, ornery, and quite stubborn.

During this season of his life, he was angry, mean, hurtful, and, at times, downright vicious. Deciding to move back home with dad was a two-fold decision. First, I was in the middle of a divorce, and I was in the valley of decision about what to do regarding my home. Second, when I saw the condition of my dad – his speaking, his thought process, the mail, the clutter, and the hoarding that was starting to take place – I knew I had to return home. I needed him and he needed me! Although my reasons were clear, moving back home with dad was not easy. When mom died, a part of dad also died. Quite honestly, he had stopped living and was just existing. So, dad was pretty much grieving and stuck in his ways. The disease, and the feeling of losing his independence, did not help at all. Every time he did something, the immediate reactions and comments from others were for me to consider how he felt.

I was often told about all the scary things that were happening to him and all that this disease was doing and had done to him. In no way was I disagreeing. As a matter of fact - I totally agreed, and, yes, I sympathized. Unfortunately, my dad and the disease continuously got sympathy and rationalization. However, what I never seemed to get was for people to pause and think about me as a caregiver. What about how I was feeling, what I was going through and what this disease was doing and had done to me, my brother, my sister-in-law, and our children? Could this be how other caregivers felt?

Allow me to re-iterate... I am not a medical doctor or Neurologist specializing in Alzheimer's. I am not here to medically explain, justify or argue why patients suffering with this condition do what they do. I am not a member of an association, support group or group with a cause. I am not here to be an advocate for the patients suffering from this awful disease. *There are countless doctors, researchers, groups, and resources for that*; I am a daughter and an exhausted CAREGIVER! Yes, I am well-aware that there are support groups for family members with Alzheimer's, and all the information and resources provided are necessary. Nevertheless, in my opinion, many groups spend a great deal of time justifying the patient's actions by providing medical facts about the disease or the nature of the disease so the caregiver can try to understand it. Again, this is very important, but sometimes caregivers just need to scream and vent! They need to sit with a group of people willing to hear their hearts and see the pain that they, as caregivers, are enduring. I am not saying that support groups are not needed or that their methods are not proven. I just want to take a moment and cater to caregivers because they need an outlet.

Thus, the purpose of this book is to support, motivate, empower, embrace, and love on caregivers. YES, this book is meant to be humorous! However, I am NOT laughing at our loved ones or making light of this dreadful disease; the cartoon illustrations are used to keep us grounded. While caring for my dad, what I realized is as caregivers we are watching our loved ones outwit and outsmart us, but at the same time, we are being told they don't know what they are doing or that they don't know any better. In this book, I want to say what many caregivers feel or think, but they would not dare say because they love their loved ones so much. For this reason, I feel they need to let it out or at least see that they are not alone. Other caregivers are experiencing some of the same emotions; so, you do not have to feel that you are going crazy. This book will include words spoken, situations, and scenarios where the caregiver has literally been lied to, hit on, manipulated, etc., and how they possibly feel or have once felt. It will include pages so the caregiver can journal their actual feelings, stories, scenarios, or humorous moments.

Additionally, it will include a place for milestones so the caregiver can list the smallest accomplishments made in some of the toughest situations. Finally, this book will provide a list of comments and/or words of encouragement for friends, families, colleagues, co-workers, etc., to say or do for caregivers so they will not only feel like they are losing their loved ones to this horrible disease but also will feel they are not losing themselves. In short, I am a daddy's girl, and my beloved dad had Alzheimer's. I loved him to pieces, but there were days I did not like him because of what he said or did. I know you would have liked me to say, "It's not that I don't like him, I don't like the disease!" Although true, statements like this are exactly why I wrote the book. In the heat of the moment, a caregiver needs someone to identify with EXACTLY how they feel because at that precise moment, the yelling, cussing, insulting, and hitting is coming from the person they love--not a disease. The thin line between literal and technical may actually mean something to the caregiver.

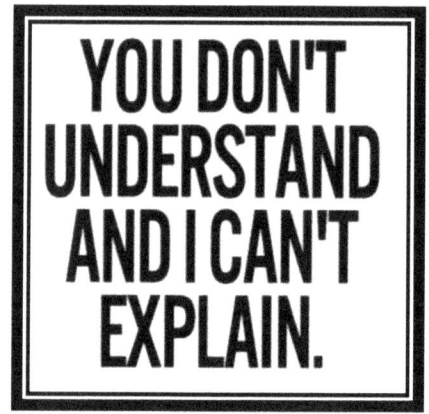

YOU DON'T UNDERSTAND AND I CAN'T EXPLAIN.

I am not certain who the author of this quote is, but it is oh so true. Many caregivers are struggling to put how they are feeling into words. So, I pray this book somewhat captures the essence of your heart and give you relief.

As for the person suffering from Alzheimer's, they simply cannot say what they are feeling because nothing, and I mean nothing, makes sense. However, I was watching the movie, THE LAST DAYS OF PTOLEMY GREY, where Samuel Jackson played the role of a man living with Alzheimer's disease.

Here is how he described it...

"I don't remember like I remember remembering, and not everything."

"It's like the things I can recollect is behind this closed door."

"And I can hear my memories, but I can't see'em or touch'em."

"He told me some things, but I can't quite hear them right."

"What if it's you who smelled like body waste, you who can't remember from one word to the next and you who got the mind of a child in a grown man's body; what would you do? And don't say you'd jump out a window cause you can't remember how to open the damn thing up- and that's how this thing is... you don't know whether to hate your condition or to hate yourself."

EMOTION 1: THE HARSH WORDS

EMOTION 1
The Harsh Words

When your loved one curses at you or goes off on you, most caregivers probably have the expression of The Grinch®...a crooked, conniving smirk with both disbelief and anger. This look is probably more intense if your loved one was a preacher or threatened to punish you if the words that came out of your mouth sounded anywhere close to a curse word. When I was growing up, cursing, cussing, swearing, or profanity was not allowed in our home; I was a PK (preacher's kid) twice over. To hear my dad suddenly using curse words was shocking to say the least. I can recall dad saying DAMMIT I guess that was not too bad, as it was spoken out of pure frustration because he realized that something he was once able to do, he could now no longer do. However, I can also recall him saying SHIT! Now that was a jaw-dropping moment. Again, this was out of frustration because a food or snack he once enjoyed no longer tasted the same. Unfortunately, knowing the reason why he was saying these words, never soothed the pain of hearing the words. You see, curse words are not just profanity; in my case, they were harsh, sharp, unkind words. Sticks and stones may break my bones, but I'm sorry - THOSE WORDS REALLY HURT!

One week, I had no help or break from taking care of my dad. There were days of struggling to get him to eat, take medications, shower, etc. To include days of hearing him say, "Leave me alone," "Go away," "I don't like you," "I don't need you" and more was like a nail being driven into my heart. These words in the ears of a daddy's girl were earth shattering. One day. I yelled at him because I just could not take it anymore. I then ran to my room, pulled the covers over my head and just cried. My sons heard me yelling and ran to find me. They climbed in the bed with me and hugged me to give me comfort because they knew I would never and have never disrespected my dad. Now I am sure every caregiver reading this will agree that we are "supposed" to have some level of understanding as to why our loved ones will curse or say whatever comes to mind-- especially when they cannot get what they want--but it does not remove the sting of the words. The reason I said "supposed" is because our loved ones have Alzheimer's. The name of the illness alone suggest that caregivers are to excuse the words, outbursts, and behaviors. Unfortunately, that is not the language of love for a caregiver.

Sadly, our loved ones can hurl off awful words and minutes later not remember saying any of it. Yet, we are left piecing our hearts back together like a puzzle. There is no apology, no admittance to errors, or anything; we are just left with hurt feelings. I recall my dad having to endure multiple eye exams and, eventually, cataract surgery. I felt so bad for him because I had my full mental capacity and could not get my arms around the pain he had to go through or the discomforting eye drops; so, I know he could not understand this. My sons and I had to place eye drops in dads' eyes multiple times a day. The drops burned and brought about major discomfort. Dad could not rub or even touch his eyes. On his lucid days, dad would describe the pain as needles in his eyes. We did everything we knew how to do to make this process bearable, but nothing really worked. One afternoon while my 16-year-old son was trying to place the drops in his grandad's eyes (in addition to him turning his head and being uncooperative), he yelled at my son and in his most authoritative voice spoke sickness over my son. He said, "I hope when you get older you have problems with your eyes and have to have surgery." My son's expression was indescribable. As a caregiver, I was not thinking about the disease, I could only hear the words. This was the patriarch of our family, a man that has been a hero to my sons. My dad's voice always carried weight in our family.

Understanding the power of words, I immediately ran to my dad and son. I scolded my dad. I said, "No dad; don't you ever speak sickness over my children again. What you said is not nice. That is your grandson, and the last thing you want is for him to suffer in any way". Dad just looked angrily as if he knew what I was saying but in a child-like way preferred to rebel. Yes, deep down I knew he was hurting. I knew he did not mean what he said, and I knew he did not fully understand. However, those words were harsh! I took over administering the eye drops, and while doing so, I begin to pray to soothe him. Shortly after eating, he calmed down. He was acting as if nothing happened, which was his reality, but for everyone else in the house, our reality was the feeling of being torn apart.

Go ahead, let it out.
Write your memories, stories/scenarios regarding this emotion

_____

_____

_____

_____

_____

_____

_____

_____

_____

_____

_____

_____

_____

_____

_____

_____

_____

_____

_____

_____

EMOTION 2
The Fist

In the movie "The Incredibles®", the baby boy (Jack-Jack) unknowingly had powers. In one, particular scene in the 2nd movie, Jack-Jack was fighting a raccoon. He literally had his hand raised about to smack him in the face when his dad (Mr. Incredible) grabbed him. This scene comes to mind because so many times I had to say to dad, "Don't you hit me!" I saw a man who had been my *Mr. Incredible* all my life, and I now saw him throwing fits of rage like Jack-Jack. What's a caregiver to think when their parent, spouse, etc., threatens to hit them? Although fragile, dad could still throw his weight around, and if he landed a punch, he would probably hit pretty hard. Dad got up one evening around 5:30 pm; he said he was going to bed. I knew if he went to bed that early, he would be up between midnight and 2am. I had already experienced dad waking up all hours of the night like an infant due to Sundowning, and I even had to cook breakfast one morning at around 2:30 am to get him to calm down. So, on that particular evening, I met him in the hallway and tried to usher him back to the living room to relax and watch a little TV.

For some reason, dad was crunk. He would say things like, "If you don't move, I'm going to knock you out!" He would ball up his fist and shake it in my face. When dad could not get his way, fighting, or, should I say, being a bit combative was his knee-jerk reaction. Dad would get this stubborn look and strong posture; it was that of a child crossing his arms refusing to cooperate. He also kept a mean/bothered look with a wrinkle in his forehead. It was our warning that he was getting frustrated, and nothing we said seemed to calm him down despite our best efforts and accommodations. Dad once found and hid a steak knife and a can of Van Camp pork-n-beans. Yes, I said, "found" because we had to hide all the knives and sharp objects. It was no different than child proofing your home for a small child. Dad loved Coke, and there was no stopping him when he thought Coke was near and that we were keeping it from him. Nevertheless, dad thought the can of pork-n-beans was "his drink". So, he took them and placed them in the living room with intentions of getting them when I was not looking and using the knife to open the can. Thankfully, I found the knife and the can. If he had these items in his hands, it would have been a tug of war.

Yes, both the fist and the anger behind the fist were real. During those moments or fits of anger, I wondered who dad saw me as. Was I the enemy? Was he really going to hit me? Why was he so angry? Where was this violent fighting temper coming from? Now I know there is

Alzheimer's research that can explain all of this, but from the mind and heart of a caregiver, all I could think was, "I am your daughter, your baby girl trying to take care of you; why are you so ready to fight me?" The threats hurt as much as the fist. As human beings, when we perceive a threat, harm, stress, or a frightening situation, our fight or flight response automatically kicks in. Yes, we all have a physiological reaction to either run or stay and fight. However, I realized when dad could not get what he wanted, it somehow triggered a fight-only response. Sadly, dad was a bit provoking; his threats hurt. They hit home. I recall one day my oldest son took my dad to the post office with him, and dad had an episode. Trying to get dad to get in the car and to calm down was a task. My son called me and was very upset because dad was talking trash, making treats, and pushing him.

Now to the average young man, dad's words and gestures were fighting words, but deep down he knew that was his granddad – the man that raised and nurtured him - he had to stay calm. My family and I found ourselves having to tame our fight/flight response because although we felt stressed and even frightened at times, our love overshadowed. We could not leave my dad, and we feared accidentally hurting him if we pushed or fought back. Again, it felt like disciplining a child. Yes, we had to be firm, and we even fussed at him. Still, deep down, we knew that this

was our beloved, and his mind/body were very fragile.

Go ahead, let it out.
Write your memories, stories/scenarios regarding this emotion

_____

_____

_____

_____

_____

_____

_____

_____

_____

_____

_____

_____

_____

_____

_____

_____

_____

_____

_____

_____

_____

EMOTION 3
The Lies

When it comes to our loved ones, the word LIE seems strong. As a matter of fact, as a little girl growing up, the word LIE was considered a bad word. We had to say, "You're telling a story," but we could never say, "You're LYING!" That was a huge no-no. I titled this emotion, "The Lies," because my dad would look right at us and not tell us the truth. Now in his mind, given the nature of this disease, that was his truth; every action was his own version of truth. I guess the added drama in every situation made it so unbelievable. At times, dad's actions were so convincing until we had to really analyze whether what he was saying was true or false. This reminded me of Charlie Brown®; every time something out-of-the-box took place, he would slap his hand across his face, which is exactly what I did. Dad would occasionally say, "I know exactly what I'm doing." Boy, that would just burn us up because we replaced all our frustration with sympathy. Then suddenly he would murmur and smirk with that comment. I know you're wondering what I mean by LIES right? Well, let's start with water.

I don't know what it was about drinking water, but my dad did not like to drink water. He desperately needed water, but he did everything he could to avoid drinking it. He took days to drink just half a cup and we had to practically trick him to get that water down. One day I gave dad a bottle of water. I stepped out the kitchen for a few minutes and when I came back, he was standing at the sink with now an empty bottle in his hand. I said, "Dad, did you just pour out that water?" **LIE #1** = He looked me right in the face and said, "Ahhhhhh, that was some good water." I knew without a doubt he did not drink that water. I started to wonder how often water was being tossed down the sink (as if water is free). Taking pills was absolutely the worst. For goodness sake, don't turn your head for one minute; better yet, don't even blink. I could not figure out how he did it. I would give dad a pill, and say, "Dad, take your medicine." Most of the pills were small, and I broke the big ones in half and gave him only one at a time. He would go through all the motions of putting the pill in his mouth (or so I thought), then filling his mouth with water and throwing his head back several times as if he was trying to get the pill to go down his throat.

Unfortunately, my dad, brother and I all have an over sensitive gag reflex; so, swallowing pills was a struggle for dad and still is for me. I think we all somehow got this gag sensitivity from dad; so, it was easy for him to play on our emotions. Most of the time, we were being gentle and sympathetic thinking he was struggling to swallow when all along, the pill was not even in his mouth (uuuggghhhh...)! Here we go again, "Dad, did you swallow the pill?", "Dad, are you okay?" **<u>LIE #2</u>** = He looks at us and says, "Yeah, I'm okay; I took all my pills - see?" He would open his mouth wide all to find out he was lying. The pill was under his tongue, in his pocket, on the floor or he threw it across the room, and later, when sweeping, I would find it. I know you are probably falling out laughing while reading this, because I'm laughing while typing, but it sure wasn't funny when I was being outwitted by someone who I was told did not know any better. When we changed dad's sheets, we would find pills under the pillow, under the bed, behind the dresser, etc. Oh, it gets worse. The same thing seemed to happen when it came to taking a shower. Dad, for whatever reason, hated to shower. We dare not even think of trying to get him to sit in a bathtub. He was quite stubborn.

We had to stay one step ahead of my dad. My son and I would take his pajamas out, get him a towel, wash cloth and get the water in the shower warm. Then we had to strategize as to how we could get him in the restroom let alone the shower. At first, we were thinking of all kinds of creative stories to get him in the restroom (heck, at times, he had us lying). Then I just said, "Enough! Dad, you don't have to shower every night, but you have to shower every other day unless you have an accident or get sweaty." Dad would go into the restroom and immediately shut the door on us. My son and I had to be quick to stop him from shutting the door in our face or locking himself in the restroom. I would tell him that I am not looking at him and that I would keep the door closed with just a crack. He had to undress and hand me his dirty clothes. Once I had all his clothes, I had to verbally coach him into the shower praying he would not fall because he became very angry if he thought the door was opening. After he got in the shower, I would open the door and tell him to give me the washcloth so I could put soap on it, then tell him to rub his body with it. I would repeatedly ask, "Dad, are you okay?" "Dad, are you bathing?"

LIE #3 = He would always respond, "Yes," but I honestly think dad was just standing under the water and telling us what we wanted to hear. I'm not certain if he remembered how to wash himself or if he honestly forgot what taking a shower was. As always, we sympathized and went through great extremes, but his uncooperative behavior and even comments made it hard to believe that he was telling us the truth. I hated to think dad was lying, but Alzheimer's patients somehow can convincingly tell a lie, and we (with our full minds) cannot tell the difference. There were countless times when dad's answers were not forthright. In some cases, we knew he would say whatever to get his way (like a kid), but there were moments we honestly could not tell the difference. It left us frustrated, feeling complex and exhausted in our emotions.

Go ahead, let it out.
Write your memories, stories, scenarios regarding this emotion

44

EMOTION 4
The Hide and Seek

By any chance, do you recall Grumpy Smurf®? No matter what game his brother smurfs wanted to play, Grumpy folded his arms and said that he did not want to participate. That is exactly how I felt when dad hid things from us. It felt like a never-ending game of hide and seek. Dad's intention was to hide it with the plan to go back to it later, not realizing, he was not going to be able to remember. Sadly, dad often lost things prior to Alzheimer's, but this unkind disease made his memory (especially his short-term memory) almost completely gone. If you're wondering what he hid, let's start with **Keys**. When dad had to stop driving, it was war to say the least. We tried to keep it simple by just locking the stirring wheel, but nothing seemed to work. So, we eventually had to take the keys. Well, once again, dad was one step ahead of us (go figure); he started hiding the keys. He hid one key, and, to this day, we still have not found that key. We had a habit of leaving the key in the burglar bar door. Dad would keep his eyes on the key, and the moment we turned our heads he would grab the keys. When he realized that we were coming for those keys, he would hide them from us, then forget where he put them.

Food was the absolute worse. While eating dinner, dad would start to get full. He would place his hand under the table and put the last bite of bread/toast on another empty chair at the table because he did not trust us to put the leftovers in the refrigerator. Dad also loved to place food in his pockets; sausage biscuits, chicken wings and French fries to name a few. His appetite was a bit inconsistent; he always asked for food but never seemed to really eat. That saying, "Your eyes are bigger than your stomach" became an understatement. Every time we got in the car, he would beg for fast food or dinner out and only nibble. I could never understand why he just did not let us put it in a to-go container. Instead, he hid food everywhere. One day I came home and found fresh coleslaw in his sock drawer (thank God it was laundry day). As for drinks - coffee, Coke or Pepsi were his favorite to hide. Dad had no understanding of cream sitting in coffee too long or soda going flat. In his mind, there was nothing wrong with it, and he could drink it later. By the time we found the food or drink, it was cold or had mold on it. Dad would get so upset with us for tossing it away because in his mind, it was fresh.

Money or Mail were the next set of items dad hid. I placed these items together because money and mail signified importance and authority, which was connected to his independence. Dad was used to checking the mail, and this regimen was still locked in his long-term memory. When I moved in and started handling everything, it was a task. Dad would get to the mailbox before me; so, he hid/lost the bills. In his mind, these were "his" bills, and he was going to handle them. Sadly, he would forget where he put the mail. Dad once put the utility bill in his pocket and went to Orlando to stay with my brother. I looked everywhere for that bill, and my brother called and said, "Are you missing the utility bill?" I said, "Yes," and he had to send a screen shot to me (long sighhhhh). Dad was used to having money but could no longer manage it. We gave him a few dollars to comfort him. He would hide it with the ultimate goal to buy a Coke or Pepsi behind our backs. Sadly, he would forget where he put the money.

Paper Towels became the next items he would hide. What was it with PAPER TOWELS? I noticed after putting a fresh roll of paper towels out, almost half the paper towels would be gone in a few hours. So, once again, I had to investigate. Dad would say, "I am going to use the restroom," but he would not come right back. One day I hid in the closet so I could see what he did after coming out of the restroom. Dad would go in the kitchen and tear off towel after towel. He stuffed them in his pockets, and when his pockets were full, he hid them in his room under his pillow. I learned that the paper towels were used to hide food and pills, but he started spitting a lot. Dad would also say his nose was running but we never saw anything. Nevertheless, when I asked dad about the paper towels, he would ignore me. However, if I caught him taking the paper towels and tried to stop him, he would get angry. It was so bad until I had to stop putting paper towels out, which inconvenienced the entire house. We even tried buying dad napkins, but he would ignore those and pursue the paper towels. It was unbelievable; I wish I had taken pictures of the balls of paper towels hidden in his room.

Lastly was **Clothes**. Dad hid clothes for various reasons. First, he had food and other items in his pocket. Anything that dad saw, he would attempt to place in his pocket. Okay dad was not a "klepto" (LOL); he just collected memorabilia or small, personal treasures and hid them from us as well as himself. Second, he had certain items of clothing he wanted to wear all the time and did not want me to take them to the washer. Third, dad wanted to dress himself his way. You see I washed and separated his clothes so the next day I could come and properly select his attire for the day. Well, dad did not like that. He felt that it took away his independence. Although I completely understood, he would sometimes put clothes on backwards or inside out. Dad occasionally wet himself or worse and did not want anyone to see so he took off the soiled clothes and placed them in the drawers with the clean clothes. "Yucky" is right because seeking out what dad hid created more work for me. Now you see why I did not like hide and seek. Much like Grumpy Smurf, Dad was upset when he hid the item, upset when he asked for the item he hid, and upset when he could not find what he hid. He would pout and cross his arms, not understanding he was the one that hid the item in the first place. This was an aspect of the disease but is very frustrating to the caregiver.

Go ahead, let it out.
Write your memories, stories, scenarios regarding this emotion

_____

_____

_____

_____

_____

_____

_____

_____

_____

_____

_____

_____

_____

_____

_____

_____

_____

_____

_____

_____

_____

_____

EMOTION 5: THE IGNORING & MANIPULATING

EMOTION 5
The Ignoring & Manipulating

Another 'ole skool' cartoon character that you may have heard of is the Grumpy Dwarf in Disney's Snow White and the Seven Dwarfs®. You know Grumpy was not always Grumpy; he became sad and upset after losing his love. Well, that is indeed the case with my dad. I truly believe dad stopped living and has been existing since my mom passed away in August, 2007. As I stated earlier, dad was always a bit tempered, but now that mom is gone and he was stricken with Alzheimer's, dad would literally ignore me when I called out to him. I can't tell you exactly what brought on this behavior, but it was quite evident when he had something in his possession that he was not supposed to have. Grumpy was the perfect expression because he would get this defensive posture and focused look like he did not hear you. I would calmly say, "Dad..." then (just a little bit louder), I would say, "Daddy..." then I would yell out loud, "DADDYYYYYYYY!" He still would not budge. Boy, it would burn me up because I knew he heard me. Sure enough, we started looking around, and soon we would find the hidden food, drink, money, keys, mail, etc.

In his mind, he had it; we wanted it, and he was not giving it up. You may be wondering why I used the words ignoring and manipulating together. Allow me to explain... To IGNORE means to refrain from noticing or recognizing. I am detailing this because usually when Dad starts to ignore, it is not because he is NOT cognizant due to having Alzheimer's. He was intentionally not recognizing us because he was plotting something. It was almost like he was plotting outside the box. Sounds crazy, doesn't it? How in the world can a person with little to no memory about much of anything still have the ability to manipulate a situation to a point that had us trying to stay one step ahead? When Dad had his plan all figured out, and thought it was airtight, is when he started to ignore me. When this first happened, I started speaking loudly because I thought Dad could not hear. How crazy did I look and sound when I discovered Dad was flat out ignoring me? Okay, I know this makes no sense without the story; so, here it goes. As Dad's Alzheimer's progressed, I started to feel as if I was babysitting. So, I solicited help from his brothers. I asked them to select a day to come get him to give me a break so I could get things done.

I would always tell my uncles -Dad's little brother and his middle brother- "Whenever you pick Dad up to take him out, DO NOT LET HIM TRICK YOU INTO BUYING A COKE OR PEPSI!" Now I know you think I'm exaggerating, but I promise you when it came to a Coke or Pepsi, Dad was a force, and there was almost no reckoning. No matter what, Dad would come back from hanging with his brothers with a LARGE cup or 2-liter bottle of soda. In my mind I was thinking, "Let the games begin." I would ask my uncle, "What happened?" They would reply, "We gave him a good talking to, and he said he would drink it later." On one hand, I wanted to scream in outrage (because I told you NOT TO buy him soda), but on the other hand, I wanted to burst out laughing because, once again, he manipulated them into buying him the one thing we were trying to control or keep a lid on. So, dad would get out the car with his brothers; wave at them; then turn and look at me with this devious smirk on his face. Now it all came down to who was the fastest and smartest. I became a strategist because I did not want him upset, but by the same token, I could not allow him to drink soda all night. The moment I said anything, he would act as if he could not hear me.

So, I decided to say nothing; I pretended that I did not see him walking to the refrigerator because in his mind he was holding all the cards. Now, I know you are thinking this is way-y-y-y-y to much drama! Well, welcome to my world, or better yet, the life of a caregiver of an Alzheimer's patient. I would ask Dad how his day was to get him relaxed and laughing. The challenge came in at dinner because if he had not eaten, he knew he had that soda. He wanted the entire bottle at dinner. Yes, he would eat a little, drink one full glass and constantly ask for more. I would tell Dad to eat and not drink, but he would ignore me because he had what he wanted. Yet, as soon as he finished that glass, all he wanted was more soda. If I did not give him the soda, it was war. So, while I had Dad's attention eating, my son would hide the remaining soda.

Manipulating his brothers into getting him Pepsi did not represent the only family members that he played or tried to play. My brother was married and lived in Orlando. He would come get Dad and take him to Orlando so I would have a break. Well, when Dad would get to Orlando, he would talk to my brother and sister-in-law about me and complain about anything that I would not allow him to do.

He could not recall the details; so, he would add to the story, subtract from the story, multiply the details of the story, and divide the story into way too many parts. At times my sister-in-law would call me to ask questions or share things with me, and I would say, "WHAT-T-T-T?" The exact thing happened when Dad would return home. I recall one day my sister-in-law and I met up so I could get Dad. The second he got in the car, he started complaining and telling me stories about his visit. If you did not know them, you would have thought he was being neglected.

QUICK SIDE BAR: In both Jacksonville and Orlando, Dad had his own bedroom and bathroom. He had a refrigerator full of food that he liked (mostly TV dinners) because he could not recall what "regular," home cooked meals were. For example, we could cook and serve Dad collard greens, yellow rice, chicken, and cornbread; he would look at the plate and say he did not want it. He wanted his regular dinner, which was a microwaveable dinner. I figured it out; these dinners provided consistency while cooked meals changed, which affected his memory.

Another example is he loved Jiffy cornbread, but as the stages of dementia changed, he did not recognize cornbread as bread. Bread to Dad was a slice of white bread. So, Dad could be eating a sausage biscuit breakfast with white gravy, but he would ask for a slice of white bread because he did not know that a biscuit was bread. OKAY, BACK TO THE STORY. Regardless of our efforts, which he could no longer understand, if we were not johnny-on-the-spot with his dinner or breakfast, Dad would say he did not eat or get anything to drink. He would accuse us of not treating him right or picking on him. The ultimate result was he wanted to stay in Jacksonville and leave Orlando. Despite the fact my brother and I altered our lives to keep him on a schedule, Dad wanted to stay in Jacksonville because that was his house that he knew very well. My brother's house in Orlando is nice, but he did not have homefield advantage. After a few questions of clarification, which he could not respond to, he got silent and started to ignore us. Later the conversation shifted, and all was forgotten until the next trip.

Go ahead, let it out.
Write your memories, stories, scenarios regarding this emotion

_____

_____

_____

_____

_____

_____

_____

_____

_____

_____

_____

_____

_____

_____

_____

_____

_____

_____

_____

_____

EMOTION 6
The Unexplainable

When Disney came out with a movie about emotions, I could not understand why emotions were movie worthy. Then when I saw the movie, I thought it was brilliant. In the 2015 Disney Pixar movie, Inside Out®, one of the major characters was *Anger*. Every time the child in this film got upset, Anger would appear as a red character with fire shooting from his head. When it came to taking care of my dad, this character became quite significant. There are things about this disease that causes our loved ones to do unexplainable things. To be honest, all their behavior could easily be considered unexplainable, but there are a couple specific things that just took me over the top. I promise if what I felt on the inside could appropriately be displayed on the outside, it would look something like Anger. Dad's room was a few steps away from the restroom. I would not even say down the hall because it was literally five steps away from his room. We kept a night light plugged in the hallway; so, if ever he got up, he could see. I got to a point where I could not sleep well at night because I was always worried about him getting up.

One night I heard dad moving around; so, I got up. I found one of my drinking glasses in his room next to the bed. I could not put it together at the time, but I later discovered that dad would get up walk in the kitchen for a glass, which was much further than the restroom, urinate in the glass, which I'm not sure where he did that at, and get back in bed. Upon this discovery, there was fire coming out of my head! All I could think was, "Did he pee in my glass?" So, now I just had to know for sure what Dad did. It was just unexplainable how he could navigate his way to the kitchen and to the cabinet for a glass but could not simply go five steps away to the restroom. For the life of me, I could not understand, why my drinking glass? So, one night I was in the living room in the very front of the house sitting in the dark. When I was a little girl, my mom had a door put at our hallway, which separated the front of the house from the back of the house, but we always kept the door open. That night, I closed the door so I would hear the door opening, just in case I fell asleep. Dad indeed got up, opened the door, went straight to the kitchen, opened the cabinet, and got a glass.

I called his name out loud from the other room so I would not scare him. When he answered, I approached him, took the glass, and I quickly escorted him to the restroom. To me, Dad's actions where unexplainable, but the next day I spoke with a friend of mine that worked in a nursing facility on the Alzheimer's unit. She laughed uncontrollably, and very calmly said, *"Oh, that's the night jar."* Now, for those of you who have no idea of what a night jar is, back in the day many of our parents experienced a time when the restroom was outside in an outhouse. Dad's long-term memory was quite preserved. So, as odd as it sounds, his mind went back to a time where instead of going outside, it made since to just go get a glass out the kitchen and urinate.

Weeks prior, I tried to get dad to use one of those plastic urinals, but pride would not let him. Once he started using glasses, the urinal was finally accepted. As for that particular set of glasses, all of them were trashed because I was afraid that the one I selected would be the one he had used (LOL). Now if you think that story is a bit much, brace yourself for the next one because now we shift from a number one to a number two.

I called my brother in Orlando who was a RN, and he reminded me of the bedside commode that we had in storage. We got the bedside commode and placed it in dad's room. I guess the urinal was one thing but putting a toilet by Dad's bed was too much, too soon. Once again, his pride could not handle that because on a lucid day, Dad was offended. He said, "What is this?" "I know how to go to the restroom" ...and how dare we say otherwise.

I cannot recall in full detail how the next incident occurred, but one morning, I awoke to feces in the trash can in the bedroom. I believe my brother and sister-in-law also had this experience in Orlando. I did not witness it, personally, but again, this is one of those unexplainable occurrences. Being that the restroom was five steps away from his room in Jacksonville and three steps away from his room in Orlando, we simply could not understand. I think the term for this was *"trash can commode;"* for me, it was just frustrating. If my emotions were inside out, there would have been fire coming out my head (OMGGGGG). Not only must I clean this up, but I also need to figure out why he won't use the available toilet by the bed or the one just steps away.

I know anger should probably not be my emotion, but when caregivers do everything they know how to do, and these unexplainable things keep happening, it can be annoying. I failed to mention the adult pull-ups. The reason why is because those were fighting words. The idea of dad wearing "a diaper" was insulting. I tried, but he would rather wet the bed, poop in a trash can or pee in a glass than wear DEPENDS. I pause here to send a big hug to my beloved caregivers around the world.

Go ahead, let it out.
Write your memories, stories, scenarios regarding this emotion

_____

_____

_____

_____

_____

_____

_____

_____

_____

_____

_____

_____

_____

_____

_____

_____

_____

_____

_____

_____

_____

_____

_____

EMOTION 7
The Confusion

Getting Dad to ask for help was an understatement. My dad was determined to keep his independence. Although I certainly understand the importance of being independent, he tried to strong arm and bulldoze pass me so he could do things himself. Disaster was always waiting for us. I specifically recall him wanting to get some bread out the oven. He did not see the potholders, and I honestly do not think he recalled what potholders are used for. I caught Dad right as he was opening the door of the oven. I yelled stop! As always, he proceeded – he stuck his hand in the oven, and when he touched the pan, he snatched it back and got mad. I said, "See Daddy, you won't listen – I said stop!" In addition to my words, I was mentally having a Yosemite Sam moment. OKAY, for those of you who do not know who that is, Yosemite Sam® is a cartoon character in the Looney Tunes series. He was a short cowboy that would go off when he got upset with Bugs Bunny. He said things like *"Now, ya racka-frackin'* or *rassa-frassin', fur-bearin', carrot chewin' varmint! Get a-goin'!"* Yep, if you say that too fast, it sounds like you are cursing.

WELL-L-L-L-L... when you cannot cuss at your parent, especially one with Alzheimer's, that is what you get. Daddy was often confused; I did my best to make him feel independent, although I understood he was dependent. It was his refusing to listen and his safety being compromised that prompted me to yell STOP! Dad did not understand what food, toothpaste, and various other items were, but he was fully convinced he did not need help with anything. We had to watch Dad like a hawk because in addition to Pepsi, he also loved Coke and would drink almost anything in a red or similar color container (i.e., ketchup, Worcestershire sauce, etc.) thinking it was soda.

This is a picture my sister-in-law sent me.
It is a picture of a spoon with an entire jar of
Peach Preserve jelly dumped into a glass with
ice because dad though it was Coke. Needless to
say, it was a task keeping Dad out of condiments,
when he wanted and was on the hunt for Coke.

If you think confusing jelly and Coke was odd, brace yourself. Once again dad was prideful and determined to do things on his own. One day, I can't remember whether it was morning or evening, I heard the microwave going. I ran in the kitchen, and looked in the microwave and sparks were flying. I hit stop and opened the microwave all to find a pair of Dad's boxers in the microwave. In my Yosemite Sam voice, I said, "Are those your drawers (underwear) in the microwave (as smoke came out of my ears)?" Dad responded, "Leave me alone; I need to dry my shorts, so, I put them in the dryer." I said, "Dad that is not the dryer; that is the microwave." I wanted to hug him because I could see the aggravation and slight embarrassment on his face due to the confusion, but he was too upset to be touched.

What many people fail to realize is caregivers are feeling the pain of their loved ones as well as the frustration from what their loved ones are doing. Imagine what would have happened if I had not walked in the kitchen. When you think about it, Dad was not doing laundry, he was trying to dry undergarments from bed wetting because he did not want anyone to know he had a bed-wetting incident. No matter what direction I turned, I felt helpless because he kept denying my help.

I don't know whether I was more upset about the undergarments with urine being in my microwave, my dad's apparent frustration, or the microwave about to catch on fire. In my mind, it is simple. If Dad would have just worn the Depends, he would not have had an accident. If he did have an accident, all he had to do was tell me, and I would wash his clothes. Now, I'm cleaning up his clothes, the bed, the microwave and trying to nurture his emotions all at the same time. I know this is not my mind but his mind, which was no longer able to function rationally.

Like me, many caregivers are letting out steam or ready to burst because they just don't know what to do. The simplest definition of confusion is both the lack of understanding and uncertainty. As odd as this may sound in moments like this the caregiver is also dealing with confusion. My dad lacked understanding of the difference between a dryer and a microwave, but I was uncertain of how to nurture my dad.

Go ahead, let it out.
Write your memories, stories, scenarios regarding this emotion

_____

_____

_____

_____

_____

_____

_____

_____

_____

_____

_____

_____

_____

_____

_____

_____

_____

_____

_____

_____

EMOTION 8
The Selective Memory

As stated previously, Dad's long-term memory would often collide with his short-term memory, but his long-term memory was more preserved. You can tell what he missed most as well as what bothered him because those were the stories he told repeatedly. He often spoke of his Dad's poor treatment of him as a little boy, his love for driving, his fulfillment in going to work, and the love for my mom. If I said, "No Daddy, you can't work or drive anymore," he would get a little loud, defensive and a bit angry (e.g., I can drive; nothing is wrong with me' I can take care of myself).

Many of you may not remember the Care Bears®, and for those of you that do recall them, you are probably unaware of a grumpy one. Well, Grumpy was more of a tough love bear created specifically for grumpy kids. So, when Dad went into his repetitious stories, I felt myself becoming the grumpy care bear. I had to either gently tell him the truth or sit with my hand at my face trying not to burst his bubble. Now, I can hear some of you asking, "Why tell him the truth? Just let him talk." Well, the problem with that is he became anxious.

Outside of the story about his dad (my biological granddad whom I never met), he was not telling these stories for fun or memories' sake. They were goals, and he wanted us to help him get the ball rolling. One day I decided to follow along with the conversation. He could not remember the name of the company that he worked for, where it was located or what he did, but he was convinced it was time for him to return to work. It was a task trying to get him to understand when I knew there was no understanding. However, it was either battle through the conversation or battle to get the keys out of his hand when he talked himself into getting up to go to work. This then led him to talk about driving.

I asked him what the name of our present street address was; he had no idea of what I was talking about. I tried to help him think things through, but by the end of our talk, I was exhausted, and he had forgotten half of the conversation. At times, I am not certain if he was really having a conversation with me or just rambling out loud to himself. On one hand, I thought, "Why bother?" Still, on the other hand, I wanted so badly to help him put the broken pieces of his life in perspective.

After a day or so of hearing the same stories, I was frustrated, and I did not want to hear anymore. It felt fruitless because he would get all upset when I could not give him what he wanted, which were the car keys. Then he would start fussing at me for getting rid of his van and him having to retire from his job. It almost felt like he purposely picked a fight with me, and the moment I was reeled in, he would forget (UUUGGHHH)!

Unfortunately, due to the loss of Dad's short-term memory, he did not recall why he was no longer working. When I returned home and discovered that Dad was not well, I also found out that he had injured himself from a bad fall in the parking lot of his former place of employment. What no one knew is that the fall was due to him having deficits with balance and movement, which are some of the early symptoms of Alzheimer's. From the fall, Dad was badly bruised on multiple places on his body. It was the same with his driving. What Dad could not recall was his fast driving, slamming on brakes, and him even hitting a bicycle. We found that out months later and are thankful that no one was injured.

Back to my grandad--there were many days Dad], seemingly out of nowhere, would start talking about his childhood with vivid details. His biological dad hurt him really badly, and my Dad never forgot. I believe some of his bitterness contributed to and even accelerated his condition, but telling him to let go or that his dad was dead did not work. The story of the pain was engrained in his mind, but the reality was not. Dad would talk about my granddad as if he was alive. After I lost my uncle (Dad's younger brother), we learned from the surviving middle brother that my dad's last name was really Lewis. Yes, you read correctly. My dad was so angry and disappointed at my grandfather that he took the name of the man my grandmother was in a relationship with. I guess in the forties, it was easy to change or acquire a name. You can only imagine how I felt. For a moment, I was having an identity crisis because *Hardy* is all I know. To find that my biological name was something else in this phase of my dad's life where he could not fully articulate the details was a bit overwhelming to say the least. Think for a moment what a caregiver must be experiencing when their loved ones unknowingly reveal a secret due to their inability to control their thoughts, and although shocked or even hurt, you must still provide care for them.

Go ahead, let it out.
Write your memories, stories, scenarios regarding this emotion

_____

_____

_____

_____

_____

_____

_____

_____

_____

_____

_____

_____

_____

_____

_____

_____

_____

_____

_____

_____

EMOTION 9
The COLD, COLD...

Dad was ALWAYS cold. Now I know this is not uncommon among the elderly because their blood is thinning, and their bodies are frail. It kind of reminds me of an episode of SpongeBob® when Squidward was freezing. It was almost funny to watch how dad would go from normal or even from hot-to-cold in a matter of seconds. You may even wonder why this is worthy of a chapter. Well, Dad wanted a heater in his room blowing directly on him. It could be 98 degrees outside, but dad was, as he described, cold-cold.

When Dad got out the shower, I would have the heater going in his room so the room would be nice and toasty. However, that was not enough; Dad wanted me to warm his clothes (literally hold his clothes against the heater) and warm towels to lay on top of the bed sheets because he said the sheets were cold. Not to mention, Dad had on two pairs of socks, two t-shirts, two pairs of underwear, and pajamas. He did not want to feel anything cold against his body. It became challenging to get him to lay down because he would throw a fit about the sheets being cold.

To be honest, some days I was exhausted from battling to get him in the shower, and then battling to get him to take his nighttime meds because he did not want to drink water. So, I was simply not thinking about heating sheets. However, once I finally got him tucked in, he would sleep through the night or at least until about 8am. At times he had to use the restroom, or he simply awoke early. That's when I had to give him a little melatonin, but this also created another small problem. Dad was so snuggled in his warmth until he was sweating. Dad no longer understood body temperature, which meant he did not understand sweat. I tried to explain that with the blankets, layers of clothes and the heater running he was going to be HOT and going to sweat.

Sweat, on the other hand, is wet and was going to make him feel cold all over again when the air hit his body if he got up to use the restroom. I know you are thinking that I am making all this up, but I am not. This is literally what some caregivers go through, almost nightly. It is the small fires that bring on exhaustion. This feeling of being "cold-cold," as Dad called it, frustrated him. He hated the sweat but did not want to stop the heater or take off any of the layers of clothes. It was a vicious cycle every, single night. Once I got Dad to sleep, I would turn off the heater, and I would then pass out asleep.

At times I think God is getting me back because I now keep a tiny heater in my room, and every now and then, I have both the ceiling fan and the heater on... Nah-h-h-h-h--that's possibly menopause (LOL) Okay, I digress. Nevertheless, it became difficult to really sleep. I felt like I took catnaps because I feared falling into a deep sleep. If he got up, regardless of what time it was, he would get dressed and fall right into his routine of wanting and even demanding breakfast when it was just 2am. Please allow me to turn into the SUNDOWNING cul-de-sac. Sundowning is a whole, different ballgame; it refers to a state of confusion occurring in the late afternoon and lasting into the night. Sundowning can cause varied behaviors to include pacing and wandering. Oftentimes, in the wee hours of the morning, I would hear something and would jump up all to find my dad fumbling around the house confused. I would have such a time getting him to return to bed or to understand that it was 3, 4 or 5 am and way too early for him to be up. The confusion erupted into restlessness, agitation, and irritability. I had to constantly think ahead, and everything I did seemed to make him upset. I hid his shoes and took clothes out of his room so he would not be able to get dressed. I even tried to alter his bedtimes, but messing with his schedule or routine was a major no-no.

OK, I'm about to leave the sundown cul-de-sac, and return to the main road.

Dad's cold saga was not just at night but was also during the day. The clothes I mentioned taking out the room included a business coat style jacket that he wore daily. As a matter of fact, I still have the jacket because I had forgotten where I put it after hiding it and recently found it. I also started carrying blankets in my car because Dad would literally sit on his hands and start trembling in any room or vehicle with A/C. During the day, Dad wanted the thermostat to be set at almost 80 degrees in the summertime. I was considering placing a lock on the thermostat to keep him from constantly changing the temperature, but, again, I was strategically thinking and started placing blankets everywhere he sat so he could wrap up when he got cold. I know these stories sound funny or even similar, but I hope you grab a few strategies and find solace.

Go ahead, let it out.
Write your memories, stories, scenarios regarding this emotion

_____

_____

_____

_____

_____

_____

_____

_____

_____

_____

_____

_____

_____

_____

_____

_____

_____

_____

_____

_____

EMOTION 10: THE LACK OF PATIENCE

EMOTION 10
The Lack of Patience

Earlier I mentioned it being a "no-no" trying to alter dad's schedule. Allow me to explain. Without memory, Alzheimer's patients quickly lock into a routine. I am not going to give you any statistics because I am writing from the perspective of a caregiver. However, during a crisis or issue, caregivers do not have time to run and research medical facts. During these episodes, we are trying to put out fires, be sensitive and think faster than our loved ones. Everything in that moment (whether we understand it or not) is based on observation. At times, that can cause the patient as well as the caregiver to lack patience. However, the caregiver tends to have more patience because we understand what is happening, but our loved ones tend to be less patient because they no longer understand. When my Dad was stuck in routine and was being argumentative, to keep from getting angry, I was reminded of Roz from Monster's Inc.® As crazy as that sounds, I would give him a stern look and say, "Daddy, can you please wait?" If you can remember, Roz may have looked mean, but she was fair and had the biggest heart ever.

I know saying a lack of patience sounds harsh, but as a caregiver, I noticed my dad did the same things all the time. He ate the same food, wore the same clothes, sat in the same chair, and wanted the same drink. Any variation of that brought on varied levels of frustration. Real quick, let me share a tiny example. As stated in prior sections of this book, Dad LOVED Coke and Pepsi. We were always concerned about his sugar intake because Dad wanted to drink sodas ALL day. We tried to give him Coke Zero, half-n-half tea, Crystal Light and other drinks with flavor but with less sugar; sadly, nothing worked. Dad knew those drinks were not Coke, and he had no patience for our experiments. He would get angry and demand Coke, and if we did not comply... well, all I will say is, "Don't leave the room or turn your head."

Time, for an Alzheimer's patient, is a BIG DEAL. In a perfect world saying breakfast is at 9:00 am, lunch is at 12 noon, dinner is at 6:00 pm and bedtime is 9:00 pm is just an approximation to gauge our day. However, for an Alzheimer's patient, those times were etched in stone. Let me explain what I call "the time saga." I recall being in Orlando with my brother. Since it was a Friday night, we decided to go out to dinner. We wanted to wait to everyone got off and got to the house...sounds simple enough. Well, Dad was ready to eat because if he did not eat on time, he could not get to bed on time. We offered him a snack and tried to explain that we were going out to dinner, but he did not want the snack because his mind was programmed to eat a microwaveable dinner with bread and a Coke. Dad, once again, had zero patience for our plans. You cannot really explain things like this because your loved ones no longer have the ability to understand and process information; so, all we really did was subconsciously irritate Dad. Every hour on the hour, Dad told us what time it was. It was as if Dad was going to starve to death. When we reached the restaurant, he calmed down because we were able to give him non-microwavable food choices that he remembered. However, as soon as dinner was over, his mind went back to time, and he started telling us what time it was every 30 minutes because now he was ready to go to bed. You know what's even more funny? He could not understand the family gathering to eat, but he fully understood his schedule and not wanting to break his routine.

Another "time saga" comes to mind when I was trying to get Dad to stay up a little late so he would not wake up early. Once again, Dad no longer understood small things like time changing. One day Dad wanted to eat at 5:00pm, but I wanted him to wait to eat at 7:00pm because after he ate, he would be ready to go to bed. The earlier Dad went to bed, the more certain he was to get up in wee hours of the morning. When I had to alter Dad's schedule or tell him, "No," there was no such thing as patience. It is like Dad shifted to becoming an annoying five-year-old. So, I would say, "Dad, dinner will be at 7:00pm" Then, he would say, "Monica it's 5:15, it's 5:20, it's 5:25; it's 5:30; it's 5:35, etc." Can you imagine trying to watch TV, wash dishes or do anything with a grown man sitting next to you telling you the time every few minutes? I, in my Roz voice, would look at Dad (trying to remain calm) and say, "Dad please stop telling me the time." I wanted him to understand so bad that eating or going to bed a little later than usual would not hurt him. Unfortunately, he no longer had the capacity to understand or the patience to wait.

Go ahead, let it out.
Write your memories, stories, scenarios regarding this emotion

_____

_____

_____

_____

_____

_____

_____

_____

_____

_____

_____

_____

_____

_____

_____

_____

_____

_____

_____

EMOTION 11
The Wanderer

During the very early stages of Alzheimer's, before we even knew there was an issue, Dad was still driving. A key indicator that something was wrong was his frantic calls about us giving him the wrong directions. Well, let's pause right there... My dad was the master at directions, a walking GPS. "Lost" was not in his vocabulary. As a matter of fact, Dad would not allow anyone to give his baby (that was me) directions because he knew I was directionally challenged. Dad knew every landmark and restaurant in Jacksonville or surrounding cities because that is what was needed to guide me home. So, when he started calling and blaming us for giving him wrong information or making it seem like the building had been moved, it was clear something was wrong. We could not understand how he could leave home and go the same direction every day and suddenly start getting lost. Dad would call us fussing and highly frustrated. We had to calm and down and go get him. In this moment I felt like Wile E. Coyote®. That's another Looney Tunes character that made eyeball rolling, exhausted, facial expressions.

Wile E. Coyote had one – twofold mission and that was to catch and eat the Road Runner, but even on his best day he was unsuccessful. Wile

E. Coyote had the craziest attempts in his passionate pursuits to capture the Road Runner--all to no end! I hate to admit it, but our entire family exhausted ourselves trying to keep up with or outthink my dad when he was rebelliously pursuing something he wanted. I specifically recall a weekend when my son and I, along with my brother and his family, all went to Walmart. I don't know whether we were in Orlando or Jacksonville, but we were preparing for a trip or special occasion. Everyone thought Dad was with the other person. I asked my brother where Dad was, and he said he thought he was with me. We soon realized he was not with anyone and had wandered off on his own. Now the interesting thing is Dad may have been lost to us, but for him he was on a mission to find his favorite things like Coke, Pepsi, microwavable dinners, etc. The family was having a total meltdown and hilariously running through Walmart screaming his name while Dad was strolling through Walmart picking out his favorite things with a well-prepared argument why we should buy it. I honestly did not like taking him to the store because at the register, it was always a fight trying to get him to put things back or even unload his pockets (YIKES!!!). Dad would get in the car and fuss all the way home about money; he said we got to buy everything we wanted but he could not have anything. He did not remember that

EVERYTHING he needed and WANTED was well stocked at both houses in Jacksonville and Orlando.

One day I was with one of my ministry big sisters, and we were heading to Sam's. On the way to Sam's, we stopped at the gas station, and we decided to walk in. While I was paying for the gas, Dad was filing his pockets with goodies. Then, he saw hotdogs spinning; so, he helped himself. I was so embarrassed. While getting the money to pay for what he had taken, I was trying to explain to the gas attendant that my dad had Alzheimer's. He just smiled and said, "It's okay." When we got to Sam's, once again, Dad wandered off, and we found him trying to get Coke. When I got to the car, my sister had purchased and was giving him everything, he wanted. I thought, "I just can't win." I know you may wonder, "What's the big deal" about this chapter? Well, a caregiver never gets a break. A simple trip to the gas station or Walmart can be both scary and exhausting. Whereas we have Wile E. Coyote facial expressions, Dad was acting like that coyote with those never-ending attempts to get Coke.

Can you handle another story? Well here we go. I got a call from my brother and sister-in-law, and apparently while Dad was in Orlando, he walked out of the house and literally got into a stranger's car! He requested a ride to the store for--guess what??? You got it, a Coke! Now, I do not know all the details, but all I know is when my brother told me Dad got a ride with a total stranger, I was done. Again, this is a man that does not understand what he is doing or the repercussions of his actions; yet, he can talk a stranger into taking him to the store. WOW! Thankfully, this was a kind person. I can think of countless things that could have happened to my dad, but by the grace of God, he did not get kidnapped, hurt or robbed. Fortunately, our wandering stories where not that drastic, but my heart goes out to caregivers with family members that wander off, get lost and require amber alerts and the authorities to get them back.

Go ahead, let it out.
Write your memories, stories, scenarios regarding this emotion

_____

_____

_____

_____

_____

_____

_____

_____

_____

_____

_____

_____

_____

_____

_____

_____

_____

_____

_____

_____

EMOTION 12
The Temper Tantrum

In prior chapters, I mentioned that Dad would hide food in his pockets. Well, I never told you what happened or what it took to get the food out of his pockets. HERE IT GOES… The food would sometimes be in his pockets for days. In many cases, he would forget, but if when he remembered, he would try to eat the food, which would have made him ill. We (me, my brother, or my son) would ask for the food because reaching into his pockets was a guaranteed smack. Even when we asked Dad to give us the food, he would immediately go into a strong posture. The frustrating reality was we had to get the food away from him because the moment we turned our heads, he was going to try to eat it. Many times, we had to just grab him in a way to calm and control him so we would not harm him and so he would not harm himself or others. This is where it felt like we met The Tasmanian Devil®, fondly known as Taz. As the youngest of the Looney Tunes characters, he was popular and generally portrayed as a dim-witted, teenager-type with a notoriously short temper and little patience. He was best known for his speech consisting mostly of grunts, growls and rasps, and his ability to spin and bite through just about anything. Unfortunately, during the latter part of

Dad's life, and due to the escalation of his stages with Alzheimer's, this became a perfect description of his personality.

For you to fully understand why I saw Dad as Taz, I need to explain what I meant by a "STRONG POSTURE". I briefly mentioned the term strong posture in chapter two, but now I can elaborate. When Dad did not want to do something, to give you something, or if he felt like he had to protect his "stuff," he would get this very defensive stand with a stern face (wrinkles in his forehead). It was a face that said, "Try me!" Back in the day, I kind of liked this part of my dad's personality because Dad was always my hero. This posture may be out of sync now, but I remember a time when this posture stood in front of me to protect me from anyone or anything. Needless to say, once he was in this mode, it was a wrap; he was tempered, strong, with no patience and ready to fight. OKAY, OKAY – back to the question of what happened or what it took to get the food out of his pockets. Well, my best answer is the day I walked in the kitchen and saw my dad and my brother rolling on the floor. Yes, you heard me right. There was a wrestling match taking place to get food out my dad's pockets. My brother who is now also deceased, was an advanced and well-trained RN. He knew how to skillfully deal with our dad. Although he was not planning a wrestling match, he had to deal with Dad, and dad was TAZ. Although he was seventy and frail, he was still snappy and feisty. Of course, Willie Jr. got the food from Willie Sr., and while it was not funny at the moment, as I write about it, I am laughing with tears flowing out of my eyes. They are both gone to heaven. Dad's departure in 2020 was expected, but my brother's departure in 2022 was sudden and unexpected. I am still feeling the pain of losing them both, but my brother's loss was devastating. It left a hole in my heart and a sting, as I never got to say goodbye.

Thinking of my brother brings about one more story that I must share. When Dad was in Orlando, he was a bit more behaved because it was not his house, and with short term memory, he felt a bit limited. However, when Dad was in Jacksonville, he was quite a handful because that was his house, and he knew where all the hiding places were. With a strong long-term memory, he was able to recall and find things even when he shouldn't have. One day he found one of his small, old guns. I knew Dad had a gun, but I had no idea where it was. Dad did not tell anyone he had found the gun or where he put it. Well, shortly after he found the gun, my dad went to visit with my brother in Orlando. To our surprise, Dad put the gun in his suitcase and took it with him. The night he decided to get it out of the suitcase, my brother was not at home. He was a nurse, and at the time, was working the night shift. Now, I cannot give you specifics, but here are the highlights. My sister-in-law walked into his room, and there was Dad holding this gun. Of course, she panicked because at this point, a gun is a gun. We were not sure if the gun was loaded, but we later determined the gun was jammed. In either case, we had a situation on our hands. So, now we have gone from having to get a biscuit out of Dad's possession to needing to get a gun out of Dad's possession. Kecia called me screaming. I said, "Wwhat is it? What's the matter?" She explained about the gun. I got on the phone with Dad and told him to please give Kecia the gun.

Remember, the STRONG POSTURE I explained earlier? Well, here we go. Dad took a firm stand that the gun was his, and he was not giving it to my sister-in-law. Of course, a wrestling match or approaching him too fast was not the answer, as the gun could have unjammed and gone off. Dad had no knowledge of the potential danger--just the fact that it was his gun. I did everything I could do, but I was limited because I was not there. We had to call my brother, and he, too, could not do anything via phone. My brother ended up having to get off work to disarm my dad. We thought of calling the police, but you can only imagine how that could have played out, given a weapon was involved. I know this last story probably gave you chills, but it is a reality in the life of a caregiver. You can do everything, lock everything, and plan everything, but you cannot possibly be everywhere and see or catch everything. These are not just our loved ones, they are our parents, spouses and in some cases older siblings. In my case, my dad could discipline me when I misbehaved, but I could not discipline him. He was and will always be the esteemed man I loved, honored and revered.

Go ahead, let it out.
Write your memories, stories, scenarios regarding this emotion

_____

_____

_____

_____

_____

_____

_____

_____

_____

_____

_____

_____

_____

_____

_____

_____

_____

_____

_____

CONCLUSION

God called my dad home to glory on September 5, 2020.

It has taken me all this time to write about these accounts.

As I reflect, I want to scream, "I'm sorry." I wish I could

get at least one day back, but I know he is in a better place. Ephesians 6:2-3 (NIV) says, "Honor your father and mother, which is the first commandment with a promise so that it may go well with you and that you may enjoy long life on the earth." I do not know a single caregiver taking on this much responsibility, sacrificing time, money, sleep, etc., that does not truly love and respect their loved ones. At the end of the movie, WAR ROOM, the older lady (Miss Clara) told her protégé (Elizabeth) that God sent her so she could share the lessons she learned as a wife, and it was now her turn to go find another woman to pour into. Well, while writing the final chapters of this book, God sent me Wakita Standifer, a daughter who is starting to experience the turbulence of being a caregiver to her mother. With every call, I can listen and share one of my experiences from my dad. She goes from tears to laughter. Then, we are both laughing; the laughter is like medicine.

With each call, she does not feel alone and gets the assurance that she is not crazy. I feel good when we hang up because she is refueled for the next round, which could literally be the very next moment or hour in the same day. THANK YOU, WAKITA! Your calls, tears and venting not only confirmed the book but gave me the push I needed to finish this project. I pray that caregivers around the world will read, laugh, and get that same relief. I cannot speak with every caregiver in the world, but through this book, I can help many. LISTEN, caregivers really do care, but we also have feelings. One of my dearest friends that specializes in mental health once told me, we must deal with our mental health so we will not become mentally ill so, caregivers also need care. I believe in the back of every caregiver's mind is the thought that this is my mom, dad, husband, sibling, etc., and if it had not been for them, I would not have life or be the person I am today. My parents sacrificed life and limb for me; so, I must return the gesture. Not to mention, if you believe in God, you are trying to honor your parent(s) so you, too, will have long life and reap good things. May God bless and keep every caregiver that picks up this book. You are a jewel in the earth. Please remember to LAUGH, LOVE and LIVE!

Things to <u>SAY</u> or <u>DO</u> for a CAREGIVER

- LISTEN
- Ask them how they are doing
- Ask them if they need help
- Ask them how you can help
- Ask them if you can pay a bill
- Offer prayer
- Offer to clean up or do laundry
- Pick up dry cleaning
- Call them to check on them
- Send a text or email to check on them
- Bring them breakfast
- Bring them a cup of tea or coffee
- Bring them lunch
- Cook them dinner
- Take them or pay for a pedicure
- Arrange a mini-vacay or spa day
- Arrange to parent sit for 1-2 hours
- Pick up a few basic groceries like bread
- Pick up a few toiletries
- Offer to take or pick-up their kids
- Come get the patient
- Say -God sees you and is proud of you
- Say -Your sacrifices are not going unnoticed
- Say -I am proud of you
- Say - You are loved
- Say - You are appreciated
- Give them a hug
- Send them some flowers
- Send a card in the mail that says, "Thank for all you do!"
- Make them laugh
- If you understand from experience, then share best practices with love

What <u>NOT</u> to do to a CAREGIVER

- Don't ask how their loved ones are doing and forget to ask how they are doing.

- Don't talk about or justify the disease.

- Don't immediately sympathize with their loved ones.

- Don't try to justify their loved one's actions or behaviors.

- Don't tell them to just be patient.

- Don't say I know how you feel.

- Don't judge them.

- Don't ask to help, then do what you want; follow the rules that the caregiver gives you.

- Don't ask, if you don't have time to listen or don't want to know how they really feel.

- Don't make them feel bad, if they reprimand, their loved ones.

My Dad's Emotional, Combative Triggers:

o Not giving him A LOT of Pepsi or Coke
o Touching anything that belongs to him
o Throwing away leftover food
o Not telling him the time
o Insisting that he bathe or change clothes
o Giving him anything that felt cold
o Not letting him have paper towels
o Insisting that he drink water
o The feeling of moisture (i.e., sweat/urine)

Our Unpleasant Moments
o Mealtime
o Bath time
o Bedtime
o Medication time

My Milestones
o I got Dad to eat a snack
o I got Dad to drink water
o I got Dad to drink Crystal light vs. soda

My Outlets
o Crying
o Writing
o Talking

List your loved ones Emotional Triggers things that make him/her combative:

- ○
- ○
- ○
- ○
- ○
- ○
- ○

List your loved ones Unpleasant Moments

- ○
- ○
- ○
- ○

List your Milestones

- ○
- ○
- ○
- ○

List your Outlet(s)

- ○
- ○
- ○
- ○

A FAITH PERSPECTIVE FOR THE CAREGIVER

At 6:00am one morning, I awoke to my dad standing in the hallway with no underwear on trying to figure out where the restroom was. He had wet himself and the floor, as he was confused about where the restroom was. Although he was standing right in front of the restroom, I helped him get to the toilet. Then, I got him and the floor cleaned up. I asked Dad where his underwear was, and in a very frustrated voice he said, "I Peed; they are wet and need to be dried." I said, "Ok, no problem: where did you put them?" We eventually found them on the floor. He hated for me to see them and wanted to hide them. I said, "No, Dad; give them to me so I can wash them." I can tell he was very irritated. I said, "Dad its ok; just ask for help. Why don't you want me to help you?" *I heard him say, "I just don't know what's wrong with me; why can't I do things myself?"* I got him settled back in bad; my heart dropped. I went to my room, sat on the side of my bed, and cried. The Lord immediately gave me REVELATION.

REVELATION...

When writing this book, I was going through FAITH trials. There was literally one thing happening after another, and I felt helpless because I could not always handle things myself. I am a bit of a "fixer." No matter how hard I tried to "make things happen," God was teaching me to totally trust and depend on Him.

It wasn't until I heard my dad say, *"Why can't I do things myself?,"* that it occurred to me how God feels when He is trying to get me to just trust Him and ask for help. For that moment, I completely understood my dad's frustration with unknowingly having this awful disease. My dad sounded like me by wanting to be independent and do things himself. I probably sounded like our beloved heavenly father-- seeing the better, easier way of getting things done but always having to fight to get me to cooperate, move out the way or simply get me to ask Him for help then wait for Him to provide the help in His way. Think for just a moment how our loved ones feel to lose something as precious as their memories. When you think about it, memories are really all we have. Everything comes to an end; that is why it is important to seize the moment. So, again, imagine losing the ability to recall the things that bring you love, peace and joy.

Synonymously speaking, I do not do things Dad's way, but I always get everything done faster, easier and with less stress, which is exactly what God is trying to do in my life. To my beloved caregivers throughout the world, just like we want our loved ones to come to us for help and to trust us to know what's best, that is also what God wants from us. This page was not a part of my plan for this book, but it's a divine intervention to help me; so, I decided to share in order to help you.

A PRAYER FOR THE CAREGIVER
By: Bruce McIntyre

Unknown and often unnoticed, you are a hero, nonetheless.

For your love, sacrificial, is God at his best.

You walk by faith in the darkness of the great unknown,

And your courage, even in weakness, gives life to your beloved.

You hold shaking hands and provide the ultimate care:

Your presence, the knowing, that you are simply there.

You rise to face the giant of disease and despair,

It is your finest hour, though you may be unaware.

You are resilient, amazing and beauty unexcelled,

You are the caregiver, and you have done well!

A SUNDOWN PRAYER FOR THE CAREGIVER
Author: Dr. Monica Hardy

To the caregiver that gets limited sleep, may God give you naps that are sweet but not deep.

To the caregiver whose sleep is constantly broken, may God keep you calm each time you are awoken.

To the caregiver that feels like explaining is a chore, may God give you an easy answer for explanation number four.

To the caregiver that can't rest from being up and down, may God send an angel to turn your frown around.

To the caregiver whose loved one can no longer get time right, may God send your loved one an angel to rock them to sleep all night.

To the caregiver that is frustrated that nothing seems to work, may God set you aside some extra "favor" perks.

To the caregiver that's exhausted after days of this, may God, Himself, hug you and give you a gentle kiss.

To the caregiver that is saying, "I did not sign up for this at all," know that God is going to reward you and answer your every call.

Written between 4:00-5:00am

<u>SCRIPTURES DURING DIFFICULT TIMES</u>

Psalms 23

*The L*ORD *is my shepherd; I shall not want. He maketh me to lie down in green pastures: he leadeth me beside the still waters. He restoreth my soul: he leadeth me in the paths of righteousness for his name's sake. Yea, though I walk through the valley of the shadow of death, I will fear no evil: for thou art with me; thy rod and thy staff they comfort me. Thou preparest a table before me in the presence of mine enemies: thou anointest my head with oil; my cup runneth over. Surely goodness and mercy shall follow me all the days of my life: and I will dwell in the house of the L*ORD *forever.*

Psalms 61:1-2

Hear my cry, O God; attend unto my prayer. From the end of the earth will I cry unto thee, when my heart is overwhelmed: lead me to the rock that is higher than I.

Psalms 121:1-2

*I lift up my eyes to the mountains where does my help come from? My help comes from the L*ORD*, the Maker of heaven and earth.*

Matthew 6:34

Therefore, do not worry about tomorrow, for tomorrow will worry about itself. Each day has enough trouble of its own.

John 15:12-13

My command is this: Love each other as I have loved you. Greater love has no one than this: to lay down one's life for one's friends.

2 Timothy 1:7

For God hath not given us the spirit of fear; but of power, and of love, and of a sound mind.

REFERENCES

Bird, B. (Creator). (2005). *John Jackson "Jack-Jack" Parr Cartoon Character*. Disney Pixar Animation Studios.

Bahrani, R., Allen, D., Culpepper, H., Navarro, G. (Directors). (2022). *The Last Days of Ptolemy Grey*. Apple TV+

Culliford, P. (Creator). (1961). *Grouchy Smurf Cartoon Character*. Studio Peyo.

Docter, P. (Writer/Director). (2015). *Anger Cartoon Character*. Disney Pixar Animation Studios.

Freleng, F. (Creator). (1945). *Yosemite Sam Cartoon Character*. Looney Tunes and Merrie Melodies Series. Warner Bros. Entertainment.

Geisel, T. (Creator). (1957). *The Grinch*. Dr. Seuss Children's Books Beginner Books

Goldberg, E. (Animator). (1937). *Grumpy Dwarf Cartoon Character*. Disney's Classic Snow White and the Seven Dwarfs. Walt Disney Productions.

Hillenburg, S. (Animator). (1999). *Squidward Q. Tentacles Cartoon Character*. Spongebob Square Pants Franchise. Nickelodeon Animated Television Series.

Jones, C. & Maltese, M. (Creators). (1949). *Wile E. Coyota Cartoon Character*. Looney Tunes and Merrie Melodies Series. Warner Bros. Entertainment.

Kucharik, E. (Creator). (1981). *Grumpy Care Bear Cartoon Character*. American Broadcasting Company, Global Television Network. DIC Enterprises.

McIntyre, B. (2013). A Prayer for the Caregiver. Bruce McIntyre Resilience. www.brucemcintyre.com

McKimson, R. (Creator). (1954). *The Tasmanian Devil "Taz" Cartoon Character.* Looney Tunes and Merrie Melodies Series. Warner Bros. Entertainment.

Peterson, B. (Animator). (2001). *Roz. Monsters, Inc. Cartoon Character.* Pixar Animation Studios for Walt Disney Pictures.

Schulz, C. (Cartoonist & Creator). (1948). *Charlie Brown Cartoon Character.* Peanuts Cartoon Strip.